Words, words, words …

Michelle Warren

BookLeaf Publishing

India | USA | UK

Presentation by *BookLeaf Publishing*

Web: www.bookleafpub.com

E-mail: info@bookleafpub.com

ISBN: 9789358315516

First edition 2023

DEDICATION

For my G'ma Yeager (aka Ree) who always believed I would and could write and publish a book someday. I think she would be proud.

ACKNOWLEDGEMENT

I would like to extend my sincere gratitude to Dr. Elizabeth Weber and Bonnie Kingsbury, professors of mine at the University of Indianapolis who helped me discover my love of writing and editing; and Kay Beard, an exceptional counselor who encouraged me to use writing as a therapeutic tool. I express my heartfelt gratitude to my parents for always supporting and believing in me, which makes it easier to embark on creative endeavors like writing a book. To all those (real or imaginary) who inspired any parts of these writings, thank you for the impressions you made on me. Lastly, I extend my appreciation to BookLeaf Publishing and the editorial team there for helping me throughout and making my musings a reality.

PREFACE

This book, my first ever collection, was written as part of the #TheWriteAngle Writing Challenge (October 2023) through BookLeaf Publishing.

The Message

Nature beckons
And reaches out
her hand
Takes away all the pain
The world is ugly
A lot of the time
But beauty is there
Just look to see …
Majestic trees
Wave their leaves
Vibrant flower petals
Dance in the breeze
Orange and red foliage
Fall from their branches
Pristine snow
Blankets the meadow
Ocean waves splash
The shell-filled sand
Tickles my feet
The moon shines bright
And so does the sun
I can smell the salt
As the riptide pulls
A stream over there
Ripples and churns

Clear water runs,
Twists and turns
The hummingbird flitters
Delicate wings
She looks at me
And then the new
Sugar and water
Taste good on her tongue
The smell of rain
Always comes
Not all can sense it
but some always will
A bunny under
The canopy cover
Squirrels and chipmunks
Run and freeze
If they don't move
Maybe I can't see
There they go
More nuts and seeds
Gathered in tiny hands and cheeks
To feed on later and now
Here comes the possum
Waddling around
An overripe banana
And maybe some bugs
To chomp up
in the cover of darkness
The doves sail

In for their snacks
Tree frogs and bullfrogs
Even a toad
Hop around looking
For flies by the road
A candy apple
Cardinal stops and stares
Blue Jays squawk to
Announce they're here
Robins and blackbirds
With red shiny wings
All around, cattails
plus lavender, citronella galore
Pansies and daffodils, roses and more
Even flowers that point
toward the sun
Butterflies visit, stop
To rest
The thicket blends
A barn owl in
The eagle perches
High above
Searching for its next meal.
Bucks and fawns cross the field
Rows of does watching, waiting
Look now at a family of fox
Playing and chasing
Like little kids
Colors bounce off

the clouds reflecting
In raindrops for all to see
Birds nests and babies
Spiders and more
Merge together
From Mother Earth
Red painted daisies
In a picture I send
"Beautiful!!
I love them!
Life can be beautiful
if we just look for it
in nature."

Twilight Moon

How slowly the dark comes down.
Where are the voices
that fill my soul?
I rock with the motion of mourning
and I'm left alone
In the night with only my thoughts.
Within my mind
storms rage rampant,
And I rise
from the last diminishing shadow.
The bleeding rose left her thorn
in me as the graveyard wind
died down.
Dionysus laughs and tips his glass.
"Another?" I hear him ask.

Philosophy 101

The night fills
with my cries
And habits break hard
each day.
Philosophers rant
and my head pounds.
Imagination is a dream
maker.
Defending the fear
of the unknown.
Illusion turns to
defense and spirals
into the soul.
The wounds bleed
thick and warm
and the bandages wrap
too slowly.
Arrogance gauges
the seeping flesh
and the emptiness
surrounds and suffocates.

The Serpent

Vodka clouds roll
in and gather me
in their arms.
Clear Eyes read the
bottle
but the darting red
lines,
like a bleeding
spider's web
tell a different story.
Another screwdriver
and the clouds thicken.
Shot of whiskey
chase it with a Sprite.
Salt and lemon entice
my tongue and the tequila
swallows it whole.
The clouds weep
Rain falls hard
inside.
Spinning floors and blurry faces
Like being hit hard
against the head,
but no pain
Never any pain.

The forbidden liquid drowns
the hurt.
Eve knew the temptation of the apple
and the serpent.
My serpent swims in my hidden bottles
and in me.
Smile to hide the fear
So no one knows
No one but the serpent
and my poisoned body.
My body tingles like a dancing flame
and I ache for just a taste.

Messy Mind

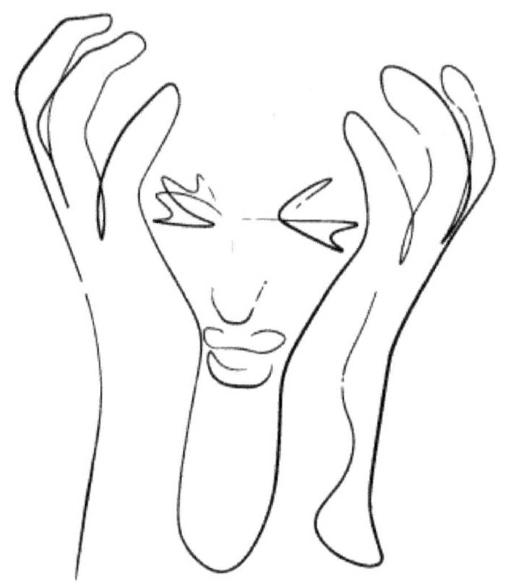

My mind
is a messy
place to be.
Maybe
I'm crazy.
I'll have to
wait and see.
The mess
in my mind
changes,

morphs,
shifts from
a beautiful cluttering
of ideas and thoughts
to something ice cold
and toxic, I'm told.
My eyes give
a glimpse of the mess
I'm in.
Sparkle and shine
like sunlight
bouncing off
of fresh snow.
Fluttering eyelids
and off goes the light
darkness now
settles behind the
hazel and pupil;
and the sadness
is palpable.
But only to those
who can see
the real me.

Waiting on Spring

My bones ache
And joints crack
as winter's arrival
pushes through
the door.
Cold and cruel
sometimes
beautiful, too.
I am never warm
Until spring's
first Robin appears
searching
for worms, pecking
the thawing ground.

Sunset

Sunset is my favorite color
Painting the sky
In gold, red, orange
Watercolor imagery
Calms my soul
In the final moments
Of an Indiana night
Revealing an end
Can be beautiful,
too.

Last Century

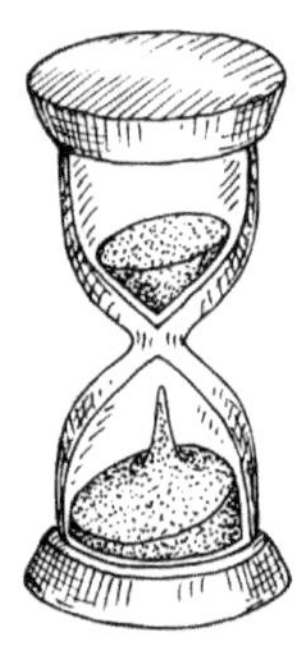

When I was a kid,
I died five times
And my mom told me
To walk it off.
Last century,
we learned
survival
skills
at an early age.
And also
How to take

people out
on the playground.
Hell, Red Rover
was essentially
a killing game.
Demolition derby
Courtesy of Huffy
bikes with banana seats
split shins and lips
more times than not.
Played outside
Until street lights
Popped on to shed
brightness through the darkness
And paved our paths
Home.

Passive Aggressive Tendencies

I feel more aggressive
Even though passive sounds like me
But watch me flip the script
Expect no noise, a door mat view
They'll be surprised when
What they see is new.
A different angle to show the rage
Quiet is nice

But it's too loud in this cage
Expectations mount
Responsibilities pile up
Do the right thing
They're all keeping count
Time to take notice and do not fear
Even nice girls turn sour
When all the sweetness disappears.

What is What

Smile more
Change what you wear
Pants won't work,
You need a skirt.
But not too long and not too short
I'll tell you what is what.
Stand with me, but do not speak
New arm candy every day
of the week
Don't say 'no' now
That's not allowed

You should be in the kitchen
A pie sounds nice
No need for shoes
You won't have time
Carrying my child
Then raising them right
That's your place now
Don't think about work
An office space
Is no place for kids
You'll stay at home, mostly
Alone
Except for the babies who
Help set the tone.
Don't speak too loudly
Quiet is the best
I've had a long day
You know to listen to what I say
Your friends have no clue
I don't care what they think
Post happy pictures don't make a stink
Nobody needs to know the dark side
Or this rage
You feel trapped, I roll my eyes
Just think how you'd feel in the dog's cage
I can make that happen, you know it's true
Your eyes aren't as pretty
When they're black and blue.
Hush now, woman

It's dinner time.
Greet our guests
And cater to their needs
You know you will
You no longer fight
I broke your spirit
One lonely night
Speaking up is always wrong
never right
Besides
You enjoy being able
To see
daylight.

February 14, 2013

She entered in full of rage
A mashup of growls,
grunts,
gurgling from the throat;
anger, rage
Twists and turns, striking
out
She's getting tired of the
glare
Then a change felt in the
air
A happy sweetness
Wiggling ball
All four paws wrapped around
To give a hug to what
she'd found
She found me, and I found more
My Joyful Jovi
evermore

My Boy

Curiosity fuels his soul
Often times he learns more than he should
Otherwise he already knows
People, places all around
Everyone wants to be here now
Ready or not, it's time to go
Rules bend but seldom break
Onto the next one he's ready to roll
Sports on his mind, always a show
Sometimes it's easy and sometimes it's not

Autumn's Arrival

The clock looks back
Just like me, over
My shoulder toward the old me
The trees turn
fiery red in the shadows
of the fainting sun.
My bones ache and these joints
Twisting like bare tree branches
in the crisp air
Fall comes quickly like going
Down the stairs, bright

Beautiful colors painted
A new season is here
Leaves rain down, hit the dirt
Reminiscent of butterflies floating
Around, but now there's a chill
In the air, A ring of resentment
dull and cold
She's a princess
Without a prince
A warrior
Without a war
Worth fighting
Anymore.

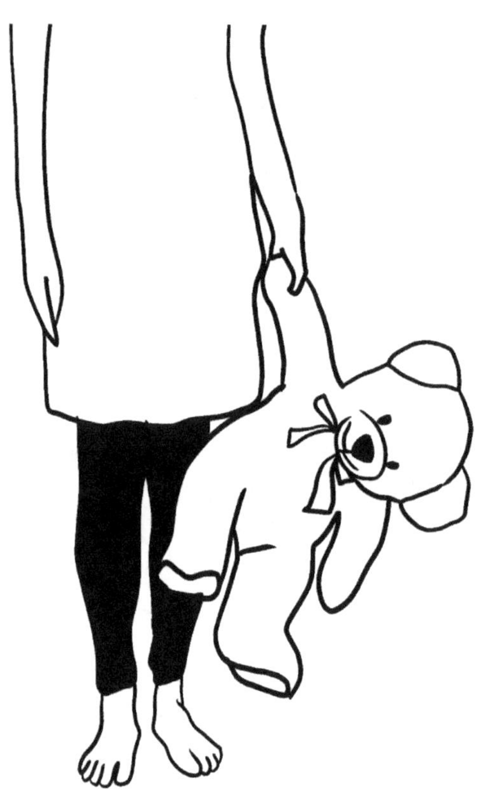

My Girl

All around the chaos churns
Violent and beautiful twists and turns
Every day a new thought intrudes
Ready or not, she's coming for you
Yes she's fire and yes she's rain
Just be patient the world whispers
Early in the mornings take a deep breath
A new day has come, a battle hymn rings
Now she's in charge of all of the things.

Memory Games

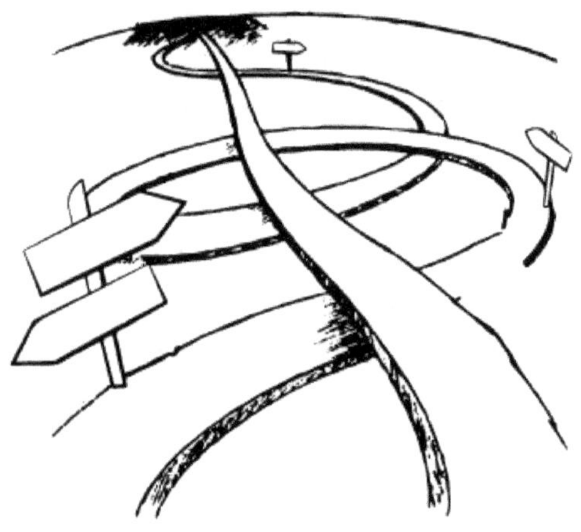

A card game, kids play
Who remembers where
The match stays? Find two
Trees and you might win
Mixing and matching won't get you far
Two identical cards must be stacked.
It was difficult then and it's even harder now
memories don't match up with what's known
to be true anymore
What is real
life, what did I dream?

Was I really sleeping or did I go
To all the places in my mind, the hallways
And staircases I see perfectly fine.
A dog and child, I think that I know.
I've been to their house so many times before
To do what, I'm really not sure.
Their names escape me
The sidewalk, the door
Into the house, these floors are familiar
A comfortable sigh, but there is no address
To match to this house. Where did I wander in
the night?
A place that exists in this realm of time
In my mind or in a small town
Maybe. Possibly.
It could be both.

Smoke

The smoke swirls around her
but doesn't actually move.
Maybe coughing busted blood vessels in her
eyes
The air feels thick. It hurts to breathe.
Every muscle pays the price.
Panic rises
in her chest, all goes black
Warmth on her face
Sunshine streams through cracked
French doors

It bounces off her cheeks, foggy now.
Like a villain in a horror movie,
the breath-grabbing smoke
always finds its way back
Doors open, quick and wide
A new perspective
Run and hide
Be careful now
wrapping her up
Cold as stone yet
Her burns are to the bone.

Sky-Blue Summers

Playground fun, like we were kids
The slide deck, cold, hard
Against our bodies tingling
Pounding hearts, breath breathes fast
Do we slide or climb our way back down?
The county cop is not amused
His flashlight shines bright tonight
Blinding light, irritated tone
Off we go toward home.
It's funny now that we got caught
Two young lovers exploring the park.

Where to next, we have time.
Midnight's tone is far behind
Summer air holds us close, a breeze whispers
Just like his touch.
Soft and gentle, never rushed.
I want candy, we know where to go.
The bright colored store with all
Of the glass. Chocolate or gummy strings
No matter what our taste buds crave
And now a movie that would be nice
Popcorn and soda to start the show.
Fingers touch then intertwine
She's drunk on his love and the way
That he smiles.
Credits roll and so do they,
Out to the car, not the hay.
Curfew creeps up, their night must end
A hug and kiss and wish in the wind.
Tonight is over but tomorrow awaits.
She drifts off to sleep, one last thought
Of those sky blue eyes, so calm, so serene.

Dressed to Kill

And really, what better way
to get close to a mark than to snuggle up

next to them, talk about the good ol' days?
Genius.
He came
pores oozing
serotonin and endorphins,
strutting like a peacock.
I was the perfect one
For this hit.
Dressed to kill,
Confident I could
Draw him near
I'd done it before,
A million times or so.
I knew what to do.
Kill him with kindness
Ready (smile).
Aim (look).
Fire (wink).

A Possum's Tale

A bowl of fruit
Rotting with time
Nuts and seeds dried
Bugs and more
Arranged
Perfectly placed
Proportionately sliced
On display
Awaiting a mouth
With tons of teeth
to bit and chew

Juices drip but not far
For fingers find it tasty
When it gets dark
it's time to feast
Night sky plus inky produce
Call them for supper
One by one they waddle
Along the fence line
Scent guides them through
the night
Curious creatures, misunderstood
But here they're welcomed
Wanted and safe.
Handsy friends
Come here to be fed.

Queen B - T1D

Hypoglycemia
Hyperglycemia
Ketoacidosis, too
You're all a bunch of bitches
Fighting for control
It's type 1 diabetes, though
Who's the Queen B
And runs the show
You're all a bunch of mean girls
Waiting to strike
You are unshakable
Relentless, incurable as well
Terminal and terrible
And knowing you is my
Personal hell
You all control me, everything
I do. What I eat, how I move
You disrupt my damn sleep
Me and lots of others

Do our best to manage you
But when you all crash the party,
It's hard to outsmart your crew
You bring blood and pens and needles
Pumps and CGMs
That act as guardians of our glucose, friends in
disguise
But they pinch and pull
and sometimes leave marks
Making our skin black and blue
They try to help us live our lives but their love
sometimes hurts.
Insulin is our life support
And helps as best she can, but she's a tricky ally
Too little or too much
Can cause chaos all around
The wrong amounts at any point
have the power to take us from this earth.
Calculating doses, basal rates and boluses,
carb-to-insulin factors, too
And sometimes the next thing we do looks like
we failed the test
You're all a bunch of bitches
You take and never give
You rob us of our freedom
But that's not the worst of it
You can take our eyesight, wreak havoc inside
Turn our kidneys and livers into insufficient
funds

You have the ability to rock
our nerves straight to their core
They burn and pinch and make us swear
sometimes you take
Our limbs
My shoulder is so fucked up
I can't even brush my hair
without grimacing in pain
You broke the blood vessels in my eyes, made
them bleed then came back for another round to
hemorrhage one for fun
You're all a bunch of mean girls
Spreading lies and stupid shit
Cinnamon won't fix this and
certainly isn't a cure
And there's so much more we get
Endless tests and scans and doctors, specialists
of every kind
Anyone who's profession ends with "igist" you
know I know them well
Endocrinologists try to help, too
rheumatologists, gastroenterologists,
neurologists and more
Don't forget the urologists, cardiologists and
psychologists galore
The costs to fight you are atrocious, you can
take it all away
Our lives and limbs and eyesight, we've already
discussed.

Add in the financial burdens
And you're really on my nerves
Already raw and firing
It gets to be too much
We are tiring
Of all the bullshit
I wish you would just leave
us alone, but I know
that's a dream that can never come true
You see your Queen B is in cahoots with big
pharma and more
We make them too much money because the
price to live is high
Insulin, that tricky bitch, is really hard to buy
There is nothing else that can do
 what she can do
She knows and they know it, too
and so some will pay those costs
The ones who don't have the means meet the
end ahead of time.
You're all a bunch of bitches
I'd prefer not to know
The sad reality is
I'm trapped in your horror show
But peace out bitches
Because for now I'll do my best
To fight and manage well
Because there's so much more to tell.

Picture Perfect

Her lungs squeezed tight by the fog
That rolls in, suffocating. Fake
interest, try and be nice.
This charade is getting old
Does everyone notice what they're not told?
Nerves burned through, annoyance
Heightened. Try and pretend that all is well.
Wasted time now is harder than Hell
Has no furry like a bride gone astray
Emotionless void where love used to stay.
Take it or leave it and she'll be okay.

Alone is her preference when she has a choice.
Tick tock goes the clock on this lackluster life
Minute by minute more of herself is gone
A blackbird screeches and cuts the air
Exhaustion takes hold
Of the body she's in
Lack of love beats
An atrophied heart.
Force a smile through
The pain, back on slides the ring
Sparkle, shine and fingers numb
The picture looks perfect
Nobody sees
The pixelation
Spread across her face.
Bright shiny
Colors cover the pain.

Paw Squad

A bulky head
In my lap
Big eyes glance
Around another set
To the left
One more time
To the right
Black and white
Mix and match
Big and small
Short and tall

They love me
And I love them
Dogs really
Are the
Best of friends

Be Patient

Lonely girl don't cry
Your time to smile is coming
Patience will save you

Picket Fence Dreams

I play
House
In my head
White picket fence
Or maybe privacy
fencing
Instead
Fill the space
Make it a home
You and me
In our own place
Laughter, music
Down the halls
You always hear me
When I call
Dog paw prints
On the floor
Scratch marks
On the door
Mailbox outside
Decorated more
Than necessary

Painted red or maybe blue
Match your eyes
And mine, too
What a lovely place
To be
At home
Can't you see
it all laid out
The best floor plans
For you and me
Following directions
might take some work
But step-by-step
Together in time
We can make
anything rhyme

Chasing Sunsets

Another beautiful
Indiana night
Sun is setting
At my favorite spot
To take pictures,
Capture the sky
In a moment of glory
There's something
About the sky and the way it
Dances behind
That gorgeous tree line

It always makes me smile
It's the little things
Gained
Chasing sunsets

Love Sprouts

Blue eyes draw me in
A trail walk and a blanket
Pull me close and kiss

Holding onto Summer

Green forms brown
But also golden
Sunshine radiates still
Flowers bloomed in
The late fall heat
Holding onto Summer
Their petals bright and
Sweet

Searching for the warmth
We used to know
The sun is shining
We can see it but cannot feel
There's frost on the patio
Furniture now
Left it out too long
Sparkling under the porch light
In the early morning darkness
It looks like diamonds
Sprinkled about
It's pretty but it's a sign
Of what's to come
Frigid temps, ice on the road
Winter wonderlands
I've been told
And I've seen
End up killing dreams
But summer's warmth
Tucked in my pocket
Holding onto summer
Through all the seasons

GenX Rules

No car seats and no seat belts
Second-hand smoke, too
GenX kids handled it all

Autumn Mourning

Somber tone
The bees' and spiders'
Work is done
So small yet important
They work and they work
And when their jobs are done
At last
One final slumber
And then many pass

Time is a Thief

How did it get so late so soon?
Days are long then years are gone
They say time goes fast,
But never explain how time
Is a thief.
Stopping and starting and
Rambling and running
Stealing and taking
Whatever it wants
Then nothing—it's all gone
The clock has tick tocked
Its last time
Once all new

Now forgotten
No one's around saying
"Remember when?"
Anymore

Agenda

Fear the witches
But not those
Wielding the match
When the fire starts
We're all to blame
There's no accountability
Anymore in this game
All or nothing
Me, mine, my
That's all that matters
Don't feed the poor
Don't help the needy
If you do they
Come for you
Call you names
Play the victim

Scream pro-life
But fan the flames
Load the bullets
Restrict our care
But don't you dare
Read that book
The gay agenda runs
The show
Just ask them, it's all they know
They argue, always the same
Sputtering only buzz words
They've been taught to say
Their lips keep moving
But I no longer hear
Chose to turn the channel
Before the first tear
Lean to the left, not the right
Stand up sit down
Fight, fight, fight
For basic human rights.

When Darkness Came

There was no light in my eyes.
Like someone flipped a switch
And all the brightness
Was swallowed by darkness.

Storms of the Soul

Whispers among shadows
The earth cracks open
Placenta falls from the matriarch
And light fades into dark
Another breath drawn
Too late
Tired eyes blink
Slowly as
Bare feet stumble
Across the gravel
Branches bend
Grab at ankles
Leaves rustle
Thunder booms
Lightning strikes
And this storm
Feels heavy
As it rages
In the soul

Seattle Rain

The sun rarely shines
On the Seattle skyline
Cold, dark and rainy
Most of the time
A rare glimpse of light
Happy and bright
Flickers on occasion
Then gone again at night
The shine is appealing
It draws you in, connects
Body, soul and mind
Don't be fooled though
It doesn't last
Lonely comes calling

Silence so loud
It's all you hear
It'll crack your mind
Splinter your soul
Drag your heart across the floor
Sweep you all up, into a pile
Leave you there to wilt and slowly die
And when you're all but skin and bones
No life left to be found
A little ray of sunshine filters through the sky
Not a lot but just enough
to catch your heart and eye
Resuscitate you back to life
A heartbeat's felt, once again
Then on que, the cycle begins
Broken dreams, broken promises
Reflect on the walls
Never spoken, never shared
But real all the same
But only in your version
Of this love game
Wait long enough
And the light goes away
You should know by now
It never stays

Innocence

"There's a manatee in my closet,"
I heard him say. His eyes sparkled
and giggled, my sweet innocent boy.
"It's big and it's nice and the water is warm."
And sometimes I join him in his fairytale world
when my thoughts
Start to swarm.
In the water everything's clear
No shadows or darkness
Creeping near. No loud voices
And no shame. The air isn't
Needed, all is well.
"There's a manatee in my closet.
It's big and it's nice
And the water is warm."

Optics

Dreams and reality
Mix together, swirl like glitter
In a Snow Globe world
I can feel you again
In my head or with my hands?
Blurred vision, take another sip
I'm drunk now, on your touch
Is it real or did imagination get it right?
A kiss longed for all these years
Played out across a crowded room

But nobody's there except you
Wrapped up quickly, your hands
on the width of my back
Forceful but respectful
Never push the bar too far
Not now and not then
Young kids fumbling around
Dreams collide with real life now
Can't tell what's true verses
Things I made up about you
Penetrating gaze through my soul
Looking out from inside
The view is perfect
It's only me and only you
Hot and hazy
My eyes can't focus
Tip the glass
Your love drips from my lips
Intoxicated dancing
In the shadows of tonight
Protected from the sun
That will burn straight through
Cast shade onto the new day
Awake now, I still don't know
What occurred under the covers
of darkness in the night
No one can tell me, not even you
It's mine to figure out
If it's not real, I'll take it still

Nothing's ever felt so right
Trusting it might be a mistake
Trusting me is chaos unleashed
Overwhelming downpour, puddling below
It's okay though, my pupils know
Gaze through the mist and there you are
Directly in my line of sight

Toxic Friendship

Sadness and exhaustion
Are the best of friends
Where one goes
The other is sure to be found
Rarely do you feel them
All alone, one is there
Then the other
One shares pain

With those it meets
Spreads it around
Like a disease
The other gives
Without care
Heavy eyelids
Weighted down
It's hard to move
Even harder to breathe
When they're with you
It's hard to leave
Try as you might
Sift through the shadows
To find the roots
Claw and dig to find the start
There they are, strong and still
Twisted around the windowsill
Try to break them, they're held tight
Fingers bleed, now there's bone
It's dark and cold and tears fall now
Grab a blanket, close those eyes
Maybe in sleep they will atone
Wake in new light, another day is here
Maybe it's one
where these friends stay home
and don't come near
And you can feel relief when you're alone

A Place in Time

A favorite place
Changes throughout time
So many versions
Through the years
Today, I gravitate
To the great outdoors
Standing in the sun
Earth touching bare feet
Dirt and grass, connect
Present and past
Reflect on the years
The places and pain
People who brought joy
And others who didn't
So many steps taken

In the wrong direction
All led back, full circle
To here, this place
That now is your favorite to be
Sunlight's warmth on your cheeks
Watch the birds, hear them chirp
A breeze blows gently
Wind chimes sing
Washing you with love
Now only felt not seen
Flowers in bloom,
Color the yard
Wildlife friends
Make you smile
Subtle and sad
But a hint of joy
Let it settle into you
Drink it up, take it in
Maybe now, in this time
Your favorite place
Isn't a place at all
Maybe you hold it in your heart
Wherever you go, it goes, too

Black and Blue Dreams

Ricocheting dreams
Leave marks
Black and blue design
Aches and pain
Thoughts and memories
Like a pinball game
All over the place
Like heavy rain
It's all too much
There's such a struggle
Ashes to ashes

And dust to dust
The light flashes
And then it's gone
So many memories
Colliding in crashes

Good Riddance

This is not what I wanted
Or expected for my life
At this stage, what the hell?
I never imagined so much strife
Through the years
It all builds up
Something good and then oh no
Here come the tears
Once again
Disappointment lurks at every turn
Regret and rage, rest assured

Are there as well I hold it all closely
Examine it obsessively
It's probably time to put the past
Over there, a place that's near
But also far
A place that we can't revisit
In the flesh
Put the pieces in a jar
Seal the lid, no cracks for air
Starve it now, let it die
Only happy memories are allowed
Everything else, say goodbye
It does no good to carry it around
Weighted down your view is blocked
Those years are gone, but new await
Let them go, be done now
Wake up tomorrow
Reinvent yourself
It's time to take back your power

Ombré Sweater

Gray turns to black
Ombré flavor
Pull the cardigan
Around me, wrap it tight
Embrace its warmth,

it feels like sunlight
"I like your Ombré sweater,"
The cashier said
"Thanks, it was my Grandma's"
"Then it's a hug from your Grandma,"
She added with a smile
Just like she said,
That's what I feel
Tears dripped earlier
An unfair fight
The sleeve wiped the wetness from my eyes
and off my cheeks
Just like my G'ma did
when I was a kid
I wear the sweater
Time after time
Just to feel her near
It makes me feel safer
It cuts the air's chill
I love how it looks
And how it feels
She wore it better though
Always did
And I'd give anything,
Put it back in her drawer
To see her wear it
just once more

Choices Matter

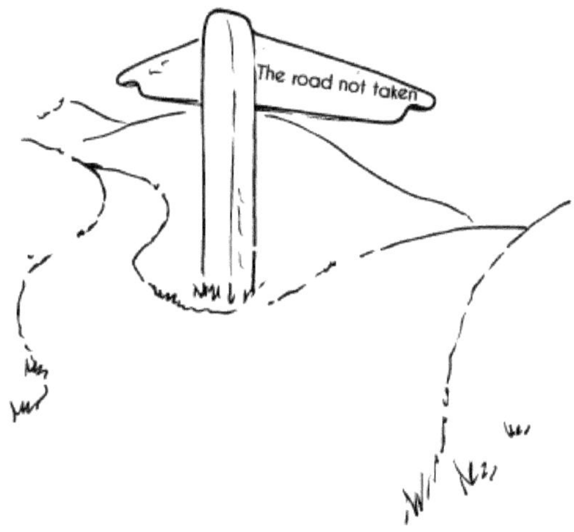

Every choice has a consequence
Sets in motion a ripple effect
Of events, washes over lives
Changes throughout time
I'd undo a lot I've done
To get back to an old starting gate
But even then, there are things I'd miss
About my current state
All of our choices lead to where we are
Right now and where we are going, next.

Choose wisely
Trust your gut
Listen to your intuition
Follow your heart
Think it through
And make your way
No better time to start
Than today.

www.ingramcontent.com/pod-product-compliance
Lightning Source LLC
LaVergne TN
LVHW051227200726
843510LV00011B/1500